SCIENCE FIGHTERS

SCIENCE VS. CLIMATE CHANGE

WITHDRAWN

by Nick Hunter

Gareth Stevens
Publishing

Please visit our website, www.garethstevens.com. For a free color catalog of all our high-quality books, call toll free 1-800-542-2595 or fax 1-877-542-2596.

Publisher Cataloging Data

Hunter, Nick
      Science vs. climate change / by Nick Hunter.
p.   cm. – (Science fights back)
Includes bibliographical references and index.
Summary: This book explores the causes of earth's changing climate, the impact it has, and how science is tackling the problem.
Contents: Our fragile planet – A warming planet – The consequences of climate change – Taking on climate change – Debates and issues – Running out of time – The fight continues : is science winning? – The climate story.
      ISBN 978-1-4339-8678-9 (hard bound) – ISBN 978-1-4339-8679-6 (pbk.)
ISBN 978-1-4339-8680-2 (6-pack)
      1. Climatic changes—Juvenile literature   2. Climatic changes—Environmental aspects—Juvenile literature   3. Nature—Effect of human beings on—Juvenile literature
[1. Climatic changes   2. Nature—Effect of human beings on]   I. Title
II. Title: Science versus climate change
                2013
      551.6—dc23

First Edition

Published in 2013 by
Gareth Stevens Publishing
111 East 14th Street, Suite 349
New York, NY 10003

© 2013 Gareth Stevens Publishing

Produced by Calcium, www.calciumcreative.co.uk
Designed by Simon Borrough
Edited by Sarah Eason and Harriet McGregor

Photo credits: Cover: Shutterstock: Galyna Andrushko br, Pedro Salaverría tl. Inside: Dreamstime: Elnur Amikishiyev 42r, Deosum 34, Steve Estvanik 31, Intrepix 37, Lcro77 30, Pietrach 36, Darryn Schneider 36-37, Eti Swinford 35, Xalanx 43, Yanlev 42l, Shutterstock: Andesign101 33, Artens 9, Jim Barber 17, BestPhotoByMonikaGniot 22, S.Borisov 15, Darren J. Bradley 11, CK 25, Sharon Day 5, Songquan Deng 21, Dja65 27, Elena Elisseeva 28, EpicStockMedia 6, Homeros 40-41, Nataliya Hora 10, Ixpert 4, Kris Jacobs 40, Jimmi 39, Falk Kienas 38, Todd Klassy 7, Henrik Larsson 25b, Wong Yu Liang 18, Stephen Meese 23, Nivellen77 26, Pick 12, PRILL Mediendesign und Fotografie 29, Uryadnikov Sergey 19, Graeme Shannon 14, Szefei 8, TonyV3112 32, Vlad61 16, Videowokart 41, WitthayaP 3, 20, Oleg Znamenskiy 13.

Printed in the United States of America

CPSIA compliance information: Batch #CW13GS: For further information contact Gareth Stevens, New York, New York at 1-800-542-2595.

Contents

Our Fragile Planet

Viewed from the ground, the planet we live on seems very stable. We can see trees and green plants, which provide homes and food for bugs and other animals. Clouds in the sky release rain to provide essential water for the plants, animals, and people below. You'll feel the warmth of the sun's rays and, without even thinking about it, take life-giving breaths of the gases that we call air.

Blue Protection
Without the blue halo of gases around Earth, life would not survive.

ESSENTIAL ATMOSPHERE

From space, things look very different. Unlike neighboring planets, blue oceans cover much of Earth's surface. The atmosphere, so essential for human life, appears as a thin blue haze around the planet. It is so thin that it could even be compared to the peel on a piece of fruit.

SPECIAL EARTH

This thin layer of atmosphere is what makes Earth unique among planets. It creates the conditions in which life can develop. It protects the planet from the sun's dangerous energy and gives living things the air and water they need to survive. If the atmosphere did not exist, or if the mix of gases within it was very different, life on Earth would also be very different.

In the Ring

Before the 1960s, people could only study the atmosphere from the ground upward. In 1960, the weather satellite *TIROS-1* took the first image of Earth from space. Today, satellite images and other measurements taken from space are powerful tools in tracking what is happening to the atmosphere and the planet itself.

The atmosphere and climate are changing. This book will explore what is causing climate change, the impact it has on us, and how science is tackling this crisis.

Shaping Earth
Earth's weather patterns and rainfall shape river habitats for plants and animals.

Chapter One:
A Warming Planet

Earth's weather patterns, or climate, all take place within the atmosphere. Weather is found mostly in the lower layer of the atmosphere, 6 miles (10 km) deep. Data gathered by scientists has shown that between 1900 and 2000, average temperatures around the world increased by 1.1°F (0.6°C). In the past, climatic changes have been gradual and took place over thousands of years. The current change, which is getting faster, has happened in just 100 years.

NATURAL CAUSES?

The atmosphere and climate can change naturally. The climate may change when the orbit of Earth around the sun changes or if there is increased activity from volcanoes. These factors have often caused climate change in Earth's history.

Warming Up
Our cool ocean waters help to keep Earth cool, but climate change is now making the oceans warm up.

THE HUMAN CRISIS

Scientists believe that the dramatic changes of the last century could not have been caused just by natural factors alone. They are certain that Earth's 7 billion people, and the gases we release from industry, cars, and other forms of transportation, are changing the mix of gases in the atmosphere and causing today's climate change.

CAN SCIENCE HELP US?

Similar issues have been dealt with in the past. In 1983, scientists found that gases used in aerosol cans and refrigerators were destroying the ozone layer. This layer of atmosphere protects us from the sun's harmful rays. Swift international action to ban the use of these gases dealt with this potential catastrophe. Can we make quick changes to deal with other newly discovered sources of climate change?

In the Ring

Swedish chemist Svante Arrhenius (1859–1927) was one of the first people to figure out that past climate changes, such as ice ages, may have been due to the amount of different gases in the atmosphere. He calculated that gases released into the atmosphere by industry could also cause climate change.

The Industry Impact
Industry is one source of the gases that are causing climate change.

The Greenhouse Effect

Earth's atmosphere has a complicated role in shaping our climate. It not only acts as a shield to protect us from the full impact of the sun's energy, it also acts like a blanket around Earth. It traps some of the sun's energy to keep the planet at the right temperature for Earth's plants and animals.

GASES IN THE ATMOSPHERE

Much of Earth's atmosphere is made up of nitrogen and oxygen gases. Most living things need oxygen in order to breathe. The atmosphere also contains smaller amounts of carbon dioxide, methane, and water vapor. These gases are called greenhouse gases because they trap the sun's energy in the atmosphere, just like a greenhouse.

In the Ring

In 1958, scientists began to measure the amount of carbon dioxide in Earth's atmosphere. They chose to conduct their experiment on Mauna Loa on the Hawaiian Islands. This is a remote place with no nearby industries to affect the measurements. Since their studies began, levels of carbon dioxide in the atmosphere have risen steadily.

The Sun Trap
Without any greenhouse gases, temperatures on Earth would be much more extreme.

Big Changes
There were no cars releasing greenhouse gases 150 years ago. Today there are 1 billion worldwide.

IMPORTANCE OF THE GREENHOUSE EFFECT

The natural greenhouse effect is essential for life on Earth. Most living things need water to survive and Earth's unique warm climate allows water to exist in liquid form on most parts of the planet's surface. Without the greenhouse effect, Earth's climate would be around 27°F (15°C) cooler than it currently is, and most water would be frozen solid and turned to ice.

TOO MANY GASES

If the level of greenhouse gases in the atmosphere is too high, they trap too much heat and the climate becomes warmer. Scientists have measured levels of greenhouse gases through history and are very concerned by a dramatic rise in the past 100–200 years. During this time, people have changed the way they live, and scientists think this has led to the dramatic increase in greenhouse gases.

Industry and Greenhouse Gases

The major change in the way we live over the past two centuries has been the rise of industry. The Industrial Revolution began in Britain in the eighteenth century and soon spread to other European countries and North America. Industry is still spreading around the world, with countries such as China and India becoming major new industrial nations in recent years.

FOSSIL-FUEL INDUSTRY

The growth of industry around the world has come from fossil fuels such as oil, natural gas, and coal. These materials were formed over millions of years beneath Earth's surface by the crushing and heating of the remains of animals and plants. Although people who lived long ago knew about these fuels, their use grew dramatically after 1800. It was then that the Industrial Revolution took place, during which huge amounts of fuel were needed to power machines and generate electricity.

Power Hungry
The electricity used by factories like this one is mostly generated by using fossil fuels.

BURNING FUELS

When fossil fuels are burned, carbon in the fuel reacts with oxygen in the air to produce the greenhouse gas carbon dioxide. When coal, oil, or natural gas is burned—to generate electricity or to power a car engine—carbon dioxide is released into the atmosphere. This alters the natural balance of gases in the atmosphere, and scientists believe that these emissions are the main cause of climate change. However, these gas emissons are not the only cause of climate change.

Piping Hot
Huge pipelines carry oil and gas across continents to where it will be burned.

Winning or Losing?
Each year, countries around the world produce around 30 billion tons (27 billion tonnes) of carbon dioxide. That number is still growing. China has overtaken the United States as the largest producer of carbon dioxide. However, per person, the United States is the biggest producer. Each year, the United States produces 17 tons (15 tonnes) of carbon dioxide per person.

The Methane Effect

Carbon dioxide is not the only greenhouse gas. There is less methane than carbon dioxide in the atmosphere, but each molecule of methane can trap far more heat than a molecule of carbon dioxide.

GROWING RICE

Most methane is released by agriculture. Rice is an important food for many people around the world, and rice farming is a big producer of methane.

Microorganisms in rice paddies produce methane when there is no oxygen left in the soil. Fortunately, over the last 20 years, farmers in China have begun draining their paddies of water in the middle of the rice-growing season. This allows oxygen to reenter the soil and reduces methane production.

Watery Fields
Rice is grown in waterlogged rice paddies.

THE EFFECT OF ANIMALS

Cattle and other farmed animals release methane as they digest grass. Meat is expensive to buy, so as the world population grows richer, demand for meats such as beef is making methane a growing problem.

Farming is also increasing levels of nitrous oxide. This is the third most problematic greenhouse gas after carbon dioxide and methane. It is released into the atmosphere by the use of fertilizers in farming.

FORESTS AND FARMING

Earth has one built-in weapon against climate change. Trees and plants in the world's forests absorb carbon dioxide during a process called photosynthesis. Huge forests such as the tropical rain forests of South America help to clean the air. These forests are being lost at an alarming rate. Often they are cleared to create farmland for grazing animals.

Winning or Losing?

In the United States, around 80 percent of greenhouse gas emissions come from the burning of fossil fuels in industry, transportation, and electricity generation. In New Zealand, almost half of all emissions come from agriculture, particularly methane released by millions of sheep.

Termite Problem
Mounds like this one are home to thousands of termites. These termites are a major natural source of methane.

13

Chapter Two: The Consequences of Climate Change

The sudden change in Earth's climate is worrying, but why does it matter? After all, many of us would like to live somewhere a little warmer—surely we'll be able to adapt to the changing climate? In order to understand the possible impact of climate change, let us consider what a much warmer world might look like.

A CHANGING WORLD

Scientists have estimated that the effects on our planet could be very serious if average temperatures rise more than 3.6°F (2°C). This would mean that large areas of Earth would become desert, where people would be unable to grow food. Many animal and plant species would also become extinct.

Disappearing Fast
Mount Kilimanjaro is the highest peak in Africa. Scientists estimate that the ice at its summit will disappear by 2030.

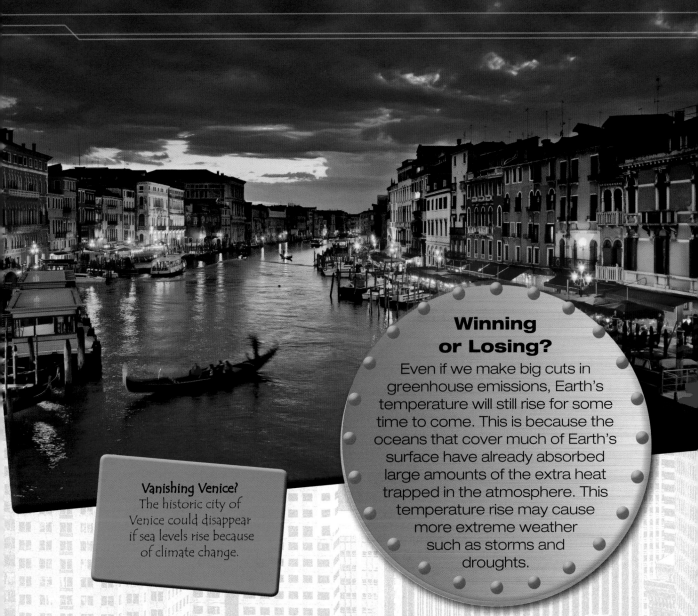

Vanishing Venice?
The historic city of Venice could disappear if sea levels rise because of climate change.

Winning or Losing?
Even if we make big cuts in greenhouse emissions, Earth's temperature will still rise for some time to come. This is because the oceans that cover much of Earth's surface have already absorbed large amounts of the extra heat trapped in the atmosphere. This temperature rise may cause more extreme weather such as storms and droughts.

THE TRIGGER

If Earth's temperature becomes too warm, it could trigger a very quick climate change. For example, forest fires would become common and would destroy vegetation needed to absorb carbon dioxide. The fires themselves would also add carbon dioxide to the atmosphere. The thawing of the frozen Arctic land would also lead to the release of large amounts of methane.

MELTING ICE CAPS

We already know that the giant ice caps, such as the one that covers Antarctica, are beginning to melt as a result of climate change. If this continues, rising sea levels could flood low-lying areas where much of the world's population lives. This would affect major cities such as New York and London, and countries such as Bangladesh. White ice caps normally reflect some of the sun's energy back into space. If they melt, this cooling effect will be lost. At this point, climate change will become even faster and it may be too late to reverse it.

Measuring Climate Change

To understand what is happening to our climate today, scientists must measure changes that have occurred over thousands of years. They have readings of greenhouse gas levels and climate data for recent years, but these are of no use unless they can be compared to past climates.

AROUND THE WORLD

Climate change does not happen in the same way in every part of the world. Some areas will see temperatures increasing much more than average, while others may see temperatures fall for some years and increase in others.

TESTING THE OCEANS

The oceans have a big part to play in climate change. They absorb heat from the atmosphere and circulate warm and cold water in ocean currents. Buoys floating on the surface can track changes in surface temperatures, while other data is gathered by submersibles beneath the waves. This has helped scientists to discover that the average temperatures of the oceans at depths of almost 10,000 feet (3 km) are increasing rapidly.

Coral Crisis
If oceans get too warm, the brilliant colors of coral reefs turn white. This damage can repair itself, but if it goes on for too long the coral will die.

UNLOCKING THE PAST

By drilling holes 10,000 feet (3 km) deep into the Antarctic ice cap, scientists have been able to take samples of ice that formed almost 1 million years ago. Scientists can measure the carbon dioxide levels in the air bubbles trapped in the ice. This gives them a measure of the carbon dioxide levels in Earth's atmosphere when the ice was first frozen.

Tracking with Trees
Each year a tree grows a ring of new wood. Scientists can track climate change through the ring widths.

Winning or Losing?
Glaciers are rivers of ice that flow very slowly down mountain valleys, feeding rivers or melting directly into the ocean. The lower sections are now melting too quickly and scientists have seen the glaciers slowly shrinking. This is happening all over the world. Glaciers are very important because they are the sources of some of the world's great rivers. Millions of people depend on rivers for drinking water and to irrigate their fields.

Figuring Out the Future Impact

Scientists have many ways of mapping climate change as it happens. However they also need to know what will happen in the future, and this is much more difficult to figure out. The atmosphere, weather patterns, and ecosystems of Earth are very complicated. When one part changes, the impact on the other parts of the system can be very difficult to predict.

Future Droughts
Scientists know that warmer temperatures will mean severe droughts, but where these droughts occur is dependent on data such as weather patterns and ocean currents.

COMPUTER MODELING

Satellite weather information and more powerful computers mean that weather forecasts are more accurate than they have been in the past. We are now better able than ever before to predict the weather.

Even weather forecasters admit that their forecasts for the days ahead are not always correct. These forecasts use just a fraction of the data needed to create a model of Earth's climate in 20 or 50 years' time. We need a better system to be able to predict the future.

PAST AND FUTURE

Scientists use data on past carbon dioxide levels in the atmosphere taken from ice to help predict climate change. They also use tree ring data. By measuring the rings on a tree, scientists can assess how warm a particular year was. They can then use all of this data, and knowledge of weather systems, to create a good picture of how Earth has responded to natural changes in carbon dioxide levels in the past.

Scientists then put this information into supercomputers, which carry out trillions of calculations each second. The predictions they produce are based on different scenarios, such as those in which carbon emissions stay at current levels and others where they increase.

In the Ring

Not all scientists agree on the long-term effects of climate change. Some believe that the Intergovernmental Panel on Climate Change (IPCC) has underestimated how quickly the world's ice caps will melt and the impact this will have on sea levels around the world. These scientists claim that cautious estimates will lead the public to think that climate change is less urgent than it really is.

Polar Panic

Polar bears hunt on the sea ice of the Arctic. If this ice disappears in summer, the bears will be unable to find food.

The Impact on People

Around the world, people are already feeling the impact of climate change. Many believe that climate change is causing more extreme weather conditions such as hurricanes, tornadoes, and droughts. Over time, climate change will directly affect the lives of billions of people around the world.

THE DEVELOPING WORLD

The people most affected in the near future will probably be those who are least to blame for climate change. Those in the poorest countries use little electrical energy and have very few industries that pump greenhouse gases into the atmosphere. Most of these countries have hot, dry climates. These people depend on their own crops, animals, and fragile water supplies to survive. As temperatures rise, crops may fail, and there may not be enough water to support them. We could see mass migrations to find food and water, creating pressure on resources in other areas.

Flood Warning
With more extreme weather, floods like this will become more common.

Desert Living
Desert cities must bring in water from far away. They will be hit hard by more droughts and less water.

Winning or Losing?
Climate change is a huge threat to millions of species of animals and plants. Deserts will spread, threatening other habitats, and food and water will become scarcer. Scientists need to find ways to help endangered species by protecting their habitats and monitoring species in danger.

EXTREME EVENTS

Climate change won't just affect the developing world. Warmer oceans mean that storms, which are called hurricanes in the Atlantic Ocean and typhoons in the Pacific Ocean, are getting stronger. In 2005, Hurricane Katrina, one of the strongest hurricanes ever recorded, flooded the city of New Orleans. Disasters like this could become more common in the future, and combined with higher sea levels, the impact could be devastating.

If climate change continues, the implications for people around the world could be disastrous. The question is, will science be able to fight back?

Chapter Three: Taking on Climate Change

The work of scientists over many years has proved that man-made climate change is happening. We are faced with alarming predictions about what this will mean for all of us. But what can science and technology do to deal with the impact of climate change and prevent it from getting worse?

Flower Power

Scientists have found that plants are flowering earlier in the year. This could create problems for animals that have life cycles that are dependent on flowers.

PROTECTING PEOPLE

One area in which science can help to deal with the effects of climate change is by protecting people from floods and extreme weather. Science can also help to ensure that farming and food supplies around the world are able to adapt to the changing climate.

Breaking Through

As the world's population grows and climate change leads to more extreme weather, people will be forced to build houses in areas that could be flooded. In the low-lying Netherlands, houses have been built that will float if needed. The basements of the houses currently sit on the bottom of a river and are surrounded by water. They are watertight and if the river floods, the basements act like a float to lift the house up with the floodwaters. The house's electrical wires and sewage pipes are flexible and remain connected even when the house is floating.

MORE CHANGE IS NEEDED

However, just dealing with the effects of climate change is not enough. We also need to find ways to tackle the causes. This means reducing the amount of greenhouse gases that are currently in Earth's atmosphere and finding new ways of generating electricity and powering our vehicles to reduce any future carbon dioxide emissions.

INDIVIDUAL ACTION

Scientists can't fight global warming on their own. Individuals and world governments need to take action too. For example, each person in the United States discards almost 1 ton (0.9 tonnes) of garbage every year. More than half of that is buried in landfill sites. Garbage that is buried in landfill sites gives off methane as it rots, which contributes to climate change. If we recycle more or choose reusable containers, we can all contribute to reducing emissions.

Flood Defenses
The Thames Flood Barrier in London, United Kingdom, is designed to protect the city from flooding.

How to Cope?

We know that even if the world makes major cuts in greenhouse gas emissions right now, our climate will continue to change for some time to come. We must find ways of dealing with the effects of climate change.

TACKLING FLOODING

Flooding will become a more serious problem in many parts of the world, either because of rising sea levels or as a result of more extreme weather. Low-lying cities will need to be protected by flood defenses, such as the Thames Barrier that protects London in the United Kingdom. This works by sealing the River Thames if a storm surge threatens the city. However, if the ice caps melt and sea levels rise much higher, flood defenses such as this will themselves be underwater and whole cities will be under threat from the floods.

HELP FOR FARMERS

Scientists must help farmers adapt to warmer climates. Growing seasons for crops will gradually change and some crops may no longer grow in the same regions because of hotter temperatures and lower rainfall. Water will also become more precious and it will become increasingly important to find ways of using water for irrigation as efficiently as possible.

RICE RESEARCH

For billions of people around the world, rice is the main part of their diet. Rice grows best in hot, wet climates. The International Rice Research Institute in the Philippines aims to help rice growers adapt to climate change. They are developing varieties of rice that will grow better in the hotter, drier climates of the future. Drier soil is oxygen-rich, which reduces the methane produced by growing rice.

Meeting the Need
Rice paddies may one day be a thing of the past. Research into rice varieties is aimed at getting more rice from each plant in order to meet growing need for food.

Winning or Losing?
Global warming is increasing the spread of disease. Malaria is a disease that is passed on by mosquitoes. It kills around 1 million people every year in hotter parts of the world. Climate change means that malaria is spreading to areas that were previously too cold for the mosquitoes to survive. The disease could claim many more lives if climate change persists.

Spreading Disease
Malaria is spread by mosquitoes such as this one. Preventing the spread of this disease is becoming an even bigger problem for scientists.

Cutting Carbon Emissions

The largest single source of carbon dioxide emissions is the generation of electricity. Most power stations still burn coal, and many are switching to gas. Although gas is a cleaner energy source, it still releases harmful greenhouse gases when burned. One way to reduce carbon emissions is carbon capture. In this process, carbon dioxide that is released when coal is burned is captured. The carbon dioxide is separated from other gases in the emissions. It is then stored underground or in the deep ocean.

WHAT'S YOUR CARBON FOOTPRINT?

Your carbon footprint is a measure of how much carbon dioxide or other greenhouse gases are released as a result of everything you do. People living in the developed world often have a large carbon footprint, which could be reduced by a few simple actions. You can turn the heating thermostat down by one degree. Or you can make sure you switch televisions off when they are not in use. Leaving televisions and other appliances plugged in when not in use is one of the biggest wastes of energy in the developed world.

Brand New Energy
Small combined heat and power plants (CHP) in urban areas can provide power and heating to homes (see page 27).

EFFICIENT ENERGY

Traditional power plants are extremely inefficient. They produce enormous amounts of waste heat and are only around 38 percent efficient. Combined heat and power plants (CHP) are around 95 percent efficient. They capture the heat released during electricity generation and supply it to homes and businesses, or use it in industrial processes. We now have the technology to build many more CHP plants.

Better and Better
Technology to help homes save energy and even generate their own energy from sun and wind is improving all the time.

Winning or Losing?

In 2007, China was building around two new coal-fired power plants every week. As well as carbon dioxide, coal releases sulfur when burned. Scientists believe that particles of sulfur have reflected some of the sun's energy, which reduces the amount of heat reaching Earth's surface. However, the sulfur's effect will only disguise the warming impact of the carbon dioxide emissions from these power stations for a short time.

Energy Alternatives

The best long-term solution to climate change is to use fuels that do not release large amounts of carbon dioxide into Earth's atmosphere.

NUCLEAR SOLUTION?

The main advantage of nuclear power is that it can produce lots of electricity with no greenhouse gas emissions. However, there are drawbacks. Nuclear fuel is very dangerous and must be handled carefully. Despite this, nuclear power once seemed to be the energy source most likely to replace coal in the future. Then, in 2011, an earthquake off the coast of Japan caused a tsunami that hit one of the country's nuclear power plants, Fukushima. Radiation leaked into the atmosphere. This accident led many countries to question whether nuclear power was a safe alternative.

Using Sunlight
Solar panels can provide power for a single house or can cover large areas to power a whole city.

Winning or Losing?

There are many renewable energy sources. The most successful of these energy sources are biofuels. These are plants that can be used to create fuel. They can be mixed with gasoline in cars. Biofuels release carbon dioxide when they are burned, but they are actually carbon neutral because they absorb carbon dioxide as they grow.

RENEWABLE SOURCES

Some renewable energy sources do not release carbon dioxide but they each have drawbacks:

● Wind: The wind does not always blow. Wind farms need a large area covered in wind turbines to make a lot of electricity. Some wind turbines are noisy.

● Waves: Ocean waves are unpredictable and difficult to harness.

● Hydroelectricity (using flowing water through a dam): This is only an option in some areas, which are often far from where power is needed.

● Tidal: Requires costly tidal barrages and is potentially harmful to wildlife.

● Solar: Works best in reliably sunny places such as deserts, where power is often not needed. Solar panels must cover a large area to generate enough power.

● Geothermal: Only possible in parts of the world with high volcanic activity.

Changing Transportation

Apart from power generation, the other biggest contributor to harmful greenhouse gases is transportation. Fossil fuels are not only used to power the 1 billion cars on the highways around the world, but also ships and aircraft.

Car Charging
In the past, electric cars have been limited because there are very few places to charge them up, and it can take a long time.

AIR TROUBLE

Aircraft give off more carbon dioxide and other harmful greenhouse gases per passenger per mile than any other form of transportation. And more people are flying every year. Aircraft have a bigger impact on climate change because they release greenhouse gases high up in the atmosphere. Larger aircraft and more efficient engines may make flying slightly cleaner, but the best way to cut emissions is to encourage people to fly less.

CLEANER CARS

The sheer number of cars on the street means that they create even bigger problems than aircraft. Hybrid cars, which have an electric motor as well as a gasoline-burning engine, and electric cars are appearing on our streets. At the moment, clean electric cars can only travel fairly short distances before they must be recharged. Scientists are working on solutions to these problems and new models are being developed all the time.

FOOD MILES

Next time you eat a meal, think about where your food comes from. Was your food grown locally or has it been flown in from the other side of the world? Even food grown in your country creates carbon emissions because of fertilizers used when it is grown, and it may have been transported to and from the supermarket. Try buying locally grown food to reduce your impact on the environment.

Going Underground
Public transportation may be an alternative to the car in cities, but it is not available in rural areas or for transporting goods.

Breaking Through
Scientists are looking for ways to reduce aircraft emissions all the time. Newer aircraft use lighter and stronger material to make them lighter, and therefore use less fuel. However, there are currently no real alternatives to the oil-based kerosene that fuels airplanes. Biofuels could be used, but at least 20 percent of the world's cropland would be needed to grow enough fuel to power the world's aircraft.

Chapter Four: Debates and Issues

There are few simple solutions to the problem of climate change. The world's countries need to take action against climate change, but many in the scientific community feel that so far action has been too slow and too little.

ONE WORLD?

In 2009, world leaders agreed to take action to stop Earth's climate from warming by more than 3.6°F (2°C). But these leaders have so far been slow to agree on action to reduce carbon emissions. The major industrial countries of Europe and North America have agreed to some cuts in their greenhouse gas emissions, but are still a long way from achieving this. Developing nations are only just feeling the benefits of industrialization. As a result, many countries will not commit to the same targets. These countries include China, which has now overtaken the United States as the largest greenhouse gas producer in the world.

Pollution Danger
Many of China's cities are so badly polluted that people wear face masks while bicycling or walking on city streets.

CARBON TRADING

Many countries have opted for a system of carbon trading. This means industries such as power generation are given a limit on how much carbon dioxide they can produce. If they want to go over the limit, it costs money because they have to buy a permit from another supplier who is not using all of their allowance. The idea is that by having a real cost for greenhouse gases, industries will find solutions.

Climate Campaign
Protestors against climate change are calling for far more action to reduce carbon emissions.

PROTECTING RAIN FORESTS

Forests play a big role in absorbing carbon dioxide and reducing climate change. Governments in countries such as Brazil are trying to protect their rain forests, which are being lost because of logging, to grow crops, and to graze cattle to feed the world's demand for beef.

Denying Climate Change

Most scientists across the world agree that people are responsible for the changes that are happening to our climate. However, there are still many people who simply deny that climate change is an urgent problem.

NO CLIMATE CHANGE

There are people and organizations that either claim climate change is just not happening at all or that it is happening as a result of natural changes. For example, some people say that it is caused by more energy coming from the sun. Scientists know that the sun's energy does vary from year to year, but believe that this alone is not enough to explain the change in climate over the past two centuries. Others say that we are reaching the end of a mini ice age, in which Earth's temperatures have been naturally cooler. But an overwhelming number of scientific studies state that people are without doubt the cause of the current climate change.

Flawed Theories?

Climate change campaigners say that those who blame climate change on natural causes such as the sun are ignoring overwhelming evidence.

Happening Again?
Climate change has happened before, such as when the dinosaurs died out. Could climate change mean the end of mankind, too?

WHY DENY?

The views of those who deny the existence of climate change are quite comforting. People are reassured to think that they don't have to change their lifestyles to deal with climate change. However, many of those who dispute the scientific evidence have good reason to do so. They include groups associated with or funded by coal or oil, or motor companies who are concerned about the threats to their businesses. These companies have a loud voice in politics and the media because they provide funding for governments and jobs for people.

It is believed that some companies have even paid billions of dollars to organizations that deny climate change and may have tried to block measures to tackle global warming. These companies do not want a world in which we no longer rely on fossil fuels.

Chapter Five: Running Out of Time

The fight against climate change has only just begun, yet there is not much time left to take action if we are to prevent some of the main problems of climate change. Scientists have two roles to play. First, it is important that they track and predict the future impact of climate change. Second, they must find ways to reduce greenhouse gas emissions—and fast.

GLOBAL CHALLENGES

The bigger of these two challenges is to stop the rise in carbon dioxide emissions. While some countries are starting to look at new sources of energy that will reduce carbon dioxide emissions, this is being canceled out by the growing industries of huge countries such as China and India. The world's population is rising and is expected to reach 9 billion by 2050. All these people will require fuel to live, adding to the climate change crisis.

More People, Less Carbon
Growing populations, especially in Asia, make the challenge of reducing total greenhouse gas emissions even harder.

BIG CHANGES AHEAD?

The other question is whether science can help us to deal with the effects of climate change in the future, without forcing people to make changes to their lifestyle that they do not wish to make. This is especially true in the developed countries, but also in developing countries where people are just beginning to enjoy the benefits of their growing industrialization. What can science offer us in the future to beat climate change?

Breaking Through

Scientists are looking for an urgent solution to the melting of ice caps in Greenland and Antarctica. These two ice caps hold more than 99 percent of the freshwater ice on Earth. If the Greenland ice cap melts, it would raise sea levels around the world by around 20 feet (6 m). If the Antarctic ice cap melts, it would raise sea levels by around 200 feet (60 m). Fortunately, although parts of the ice caps are melting, they are also being added to by new snowfall.

Hot Spot Antarctica
Temperatures in parts of Antarctica are rising faster than anywhere else on Earth.

Future Technologies

New technologies and discoveries have solved many problems that people have faced in the past, from inventing amazing machines to curing diseases. Will science be able to now create technologies to win the war on climate change?

No Gas Needed
Solar cookers such as this one can mean that people in remote parts of the world do not have to cut down trees to make fires.

HOPE FOR THE FUTURE

Climate-change scientists believe that by 2050, 80 percent of our energy could be produced from renewable sources. This target requires global political action to ensure it happens. Some renewable sources such as solar power plants are growing quickly but others, such as wave technology, are less well advanced. Although renewable energies only make up a small part of the world's energy supply, this is changing. Between 2008 and 2009, almost half of all new electricity-generating projects used renewable sources.

SPACE-AGE SOLUTIONS

Other technologies are still many years away. One idea is to create huge reflective panels in space that would prevent some of the sun's energy from reaching Earth. Other more futuristic ideas include the creation of huge machines that could absorb carbon dioxide from the atmosphere. Others suggest covering huge portions of the planet with reflective films, which would reflect the sun's energy back out into space. Some have even proposed fertilizing the oceans so that phytoplankton (tiny ocean plants) will grow in number and absorb more carbon dioxide. However, the side effects of these solutions could be dangerous and unpredictable.

Experts believe that many of these technologies, if they work at all, are too far in the future to deliver the cut in greenhouse gas emissions that we need now. In the future, the world will also have to reduce energy use and deal with the effects of climate change.

Answers in Space?
Solutions such as reflecting the sun's energy in space are untested and far into the future.

Breaking Through

Major volcanic eruptions release particles into the atmosphere. Some of these particles, such as sulfur, can help to reflect the sun's heat back out into space. Some scientists favor releasing such particles into the atmosphere to combat climate change, but no one really knows what other effects this might have on Earth's atmosphere and climate.

Dealing with the Effects

The effects of climate change will include more extreme weather in the years to come, from powerful storms and heavy rainfall for some to longer periods of drought for others. Scientists now need to develop more accurate systems for predicting both immediate and long-term changes.

Water Worry
Finding ways to preserve or reuse water is likely to be a major issue in the future. Already, many millions of people do not have access to clean water.

THE FIGHT FOR WATER

Prolonged drought will make water an even more precious resource for Earth's growing population. In some parts of the world where water is already scarce, salt is removed from seawater so it can be used for drinking and irrigation. This may become more widespread.

Forced to Leave
If they cannot grow crops, many people will be forced to leave their homes and become refugees in search of food. Crop research can help to prevent this.

Breaking Through

Would you eat a burger grown in a laboratory from cow stem cells? It may not sound great but it could be a weapon in the battle against climate change. Meat grown in this way would release a fraction of the greenhouse gases given off and energy used by cattle. It could one day even satisfy the world's growing demand for meat without costing Earth too much.

Moving Ahead
The next step from GM foods may be synthetic biology, in which new plants that absorb more carbon dioxide are developed.

GENETIC MODIFICATION

All living things need water, including the crops we grow for food. Genetically modified (GM) crops could help to provide enough food in the future. Genetic material in these crops is changed so the plants can grow in hotter climates or use less water. Some GM crops are even resistant to pests, which means that greenhouse-gas–producing pesticides and fertilizers would not be needed for these crops.

People who are against GM crops say that the technology is dangerous. They believe that GM crops could change the way ecosystems operate.

Another problem is that trees are being developed that contain more of the cellulose needed to produce biofuels. However, to create forests of these trees will require large areas of land. This may mean that endangered forests are cleared and the animal and plant species in them will suffer.

The Fight Continues: Is Science Winning?

Dealing with climate change is now a major issue for the world's leaders. This is a small victory for the scientists who have spent so long gathering data and warning of the possible impact of climate change. However, the biggest battles still lie ahead.

Science has developed many weapons in the battle against climate change. Research into renewable energy sources is providing real alternatives to the world's fossil fuel use. Future advances in areas such as carbon capture and the genetic modification of crops could also help in this fight.

Healthy Fixes
Combating climate change is not all about new technology. Bicycling and walking for short distances make us healthier and releases much less carbon dioxide than taking the car.

MAKING THE RIGHT CHOICES NOW

Science can give us the technology to win the fight against climate change, but scientists cannot force people to take action. To stop climate change, industries across the world need to adopt clean sources of energy. People in developed countries will also have to change their lifestyles to use less energy. For this to happen, all governments need to work with scientists around the world in the fight against climate change.

GLOBAL PRESSURE

The world's tropical rain forests absorb massive quantities of carbon dioxide during photosynthesis. As a result of increasing awareness of climate change, between 2000 and 2010 the rate at which these forests were being cut down dropped by 25 percent. Despite this, in every year during this period, an area around twice the size of the state of Massachusetts was still lost in the world's three biggest rain forests.

Breaking Through

Photosynthesis is the process during which plants use sunlight to convert carbon dioxide into energy and oxygen. Scientists are developing a similar process that could enable us to convert carbon dioxide in the atmosphere into various fuels and hope to use solar energy to release hydrogen from water. Hydrogen could then be used as a fuel. In 2012, Swedish scientists announced a breakthrough in their research that could make this revolutionary technology a reality.

Food Fight

GM crops may help us to deal with climate change, but many people believe they will create new problems.

The Climate Story

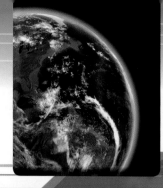

1800
Carbon dioxide is present in the atmosphere at concentrations of around 290 particles per million (ppm).

1882
Thomas Edison opens the first electric power station in New York City. It is used to power the electric lightbulbs invented by Edison.

1896
Svante Arrhenius publishes the first calculation of human impact on climate change.

1908
Henry Ford produces the Model T, the first mass-produced car for ordinary families.

1958
Studies show that the greenhouse effect on Venus is responsible for very high temperatures on the planet's surface.

2002
The 1,254-square-mile (3,250-square-km) Larsen B ice shelf breaks away from Antarctica and melts in the Southern Ocean.

2004
A study in the journal *Nature* predicts that more than half of all animals and plant species could be extinct by 2050.

2005
Hurricane Katrina strikes New Orleans, leading to public debate about the impact of climate change on extreme weather.

2007
The fourth IPCC report warns that serious effects of global warming are being seen and that the cost of cutting carbon emissions would be far less than the cost of dealing with consequences of continuing climate change.

2007
Former Vice President Al Gore and the IPCC receive the Nobel Peace Prize for their campaigns to raise awareness of climate change.

1960
US scientist Charles Keeling accurately measures carbon dioxide in the atmosphere at 315 ppm.

1970
The first Earth Day takes place to highlight the world's environmental issues.

1988
IPCC is formed by United Nations to assess the progress and impact of global warming.

1989
Fossil fuel producers and other industries form the Global Climate Coalition to spread their message that evidence on climate change is too weak to justify any urgent action.

1997
The Kyoto Protocol is agreed in Japan. Many developed countries agree to cuts in greenhouse gas emissions. However, the agreement is rejected by the United States.

2009
The Copenhagen climate change conference fails to agree on limits on greenhouse gas emissions.

2010
The warmest year ever is recorded; although if scientists' predictions are correct, this record will soon be beaten.

2011
Levels of atmospheric carbon dioxide reach 395 ppm, the highest level ever recorded. Scientists warn that levels need to stay close to 400 ppm if the world is to have any chance of avoiding serious climate change.

Glossary

atmosphere a layer of gases surrounding Earth

biofuels fuels made from plant material

carbon dioxide a greenhouse gas that is released when fossil fuels and organic matter are burned

carbon neutral describing fuels that neither add to nor take away from the amount of carbon dioxide present in the atmosphere

developed countries rich, industrialized countries where the economy is fully developed, such as the countries of North America and Europe

developing countries countries in which the economy is not yet fully developed, including many countries in Africa, Asia, and South America

drought a period with little or no rainfall, leading to water shortages

ecosystem the environment and the plants and animals in it

endangered species a type of animal or plant that is under threat of becoming extinct

extinct when a species has completely died out

fertilizer a natural or man-made substance added to soil to make crops grow better

fossil fuel an energy source formed from the decayed remains of living things, including coal, oil, and natural gas

generate to convert one form of energy into another, for example to produce electricity

genetically modified (GM) the use of biotechnology to change the genes of an organism to give it different properties

greenhouse effect the process by which greenhouse gases trap the sun's heat to warm Earth

greenhouse gas gases that trap heat in the atmosphere

hurricane a powerful tropical storm with very strong swirling winds and powerful waves

ice age an era when Earth's climate was much colder than it is now and ice covered large parts of the planet

Industrial Revolution the major development of industry in a country. The Industrial Revolution began in Europe in the eighteenth century

industrialization the development of industries on a large scale

irrigate to channel rain and floodwaters to help crops grow

methane a greenhouse gas that is released when materials rot

migration a journey from one place to another, for example to live in a new country

molecule a group of atoms held together by chemical bonds

ozone layer the layer of ozone (a form of oxygen) high in the atmosphere that protects Earth from the sun's harmful rays

pesticide a chemical that is sprayed on crops to kill insects and other pests that attack them

photosynthesis the process by which plants use sunlight to make food from carbon dioxide and water, absorbing carbon dioxide from the atmosphere

radiation harmful particles emitted by materials used in nuclear power generation

renewable an energy source that will not run out

rice paddies very wet fields in which rice is grown

solar power energy that comes from the sun

stem cell a living cell that can be used by scientists to grow new living tissue

submersible a vehicle that operates underwater

turbine a motor, driven by steam or water power, that generates electricity

For More Information

BOOKS

Dell, Pamela. *Protecting the Planet: Environmental Activism*. Minneapolis, MN: Compass Point Books, 2010.

Hartman, Eve, and Wendy Meshbesher. *Climate Change*. Chicago, IL: Raintree, 2010.

Spilsbury, Richard. *Climate Change Catastrophe*. New York, NY: Rosen Central, 2010.

Woodward, John. *Eyewitness Climate Change*. New York, NY: Dorling Kindersley, 2008.

WEBSITES

Visit the Friends of the Earth website for the latest news on action on climate change and other issues:
www.foei.org

Use the resources on this website to find out all about climate change and even calculate your impact on the environment:
www.epa.gov/climatechange/kids

Find games, activities, questions, and information on climate change at NASA's climate change site for young people at:
climate.nasa.gov/kids

Publisher's note to educators and parents: Our editors have carefully reviewed these websites to ensure that they are suitable for students. Many websites change frequently, however, and we cannot guarantee that a site's future contents will continue to meet our high standards of quality and educational value. Be advised that students should be closely supervised whenever they access the Internet.

Index